THUNDER AT DARWIN STATION

LANCE STRATE

NeoPoiesisPress.com

NeoPoiesis Press, LLC

2775 Harbor Ave SW, Suite D, Seattle, WA 98126-2138

Inquiries: Info@ NeoPoiesisPress.com

NeoPoiesisPress.com

Lance Strate – Thunder at Darwin Station
ISBN 9780989201872 (pbk)

    1. Poetry. I. Strate, Lance. II. Thunder at Darwin Station.

Library of Congress Control Number: 2014943016

First Edition

Design, art direction and typography: Milo Duffin and Stephen Roxborough
Cover illustration: Sheffield Abella

Printed in the United States of America

for the DarWin (or lose)

this book is dedicated to my long lost friends

and our MySpace poetry community

wiped out by an online extinction event

of epic proportions

Table of Contents

Ty ran a sore loser off the field
lounge lizard living la vida dolorosa

says
          baby do you come here often?

says
          you must be a fossil, babe
              because I dig you!

origin of the specious
a line of slow descent
the passion
the way

              don't cross me baby
              don't shoot me down
              the cavalry is coming, babe
              no, no, I ain't joshing you
              survival of the fit test the battle
              so let's go jerry commando
              sow while dotes
              and sects you'll know'll
              reap production

and me, I just have to ask:

          is it just a random mutation
              that brings you here tonight?

is it acquired traits passed down
  a remarkable adaptation?

does the crew see fiction
  or faction in your story?

do you see just in theory?
  Thee receive me?
  do you see me?

have I changed so much?
  have I evolved?
  am I reborn for you?

I won't kiss and teleologically tell your theology

  No O Sphere!
  No O Globe!
  No O Gaia
    my mother
    my lover divine!

Let that meaty ore strike us down
  and we will go quietly into the long night
between instinct and extinct
  we will hold lightning in a bottle
and a mighty roar will echo
  across the eons and ions:

Say *Shazam* now
let's transform now
say it with me
say it now
say it ten times
ten times over
say *Shazam* now
say it now!

reach your plateau
and I'll be waiting
at the station
with punctual equilibrium

      I'll be waiting there for you
      I'll be waiting at the station, babe
      I'll be waiting there for you

when the very last train's leaving town

Scoping out the trials
  and errors
    that brought us to
      the brink. Is it
        evil you shun?

      Standing on the edge
        of Eden's river
      you stare...
    Searching for
the one?

Do you fear the grave mother
  who buries us all?
    Do you resist her embrace?
    Do you turn from her face?

      The current flows inside your head
        your reptile brain is roaring red
      but is it anger
    or just appetite
that keeps you in your place?

Bloodline manqué
  climbing up
    your family tree
      a clinging I.V. divine?
        Or a poison cup of wine?

      Is it blues that you bleed
        for your once-noble breed?

Do your ancestors cry out
in apish dissent?

Swinging from the branches
   going out on a limb
      is the weight too much to bear?
         Do you even have a prayer?

         Take communion with eukaryotes
      and sing amoebal hymns on high
   to the glory and the mystery
of our divine chemistry
to Life in all its variety
   and that will suffice for piety

Thomas Henry said to Charles,
"I will be your bulldog, Sir!
Steadfast and unwavering,
Faithful and true,
Loyal to a fault;
I shall not falter,
Neither shall I loose my grip
As we progress,
Side by side,
Shoulder to shoulder,
Arm in arm,
To arms!
Onward Soldiers of Science,
Marching as to war!
A Selective Service most natural,
Fit to survive the Jerichonian fight!
So sound the horns!
Signal the attack!
Let the great trumpets trill and blast!
Hear the deep rumble
Leading to awe-filled ascent, O Man!
Tremors of transformation
Give rise to a terrible wail,
As brick and mortar shake and crumble,
As we call down the walls of ignorance,
With a word!
Change!
Change is the only constant
Good comrade Charles!
Change shall be our legacy, and inheritance!

And my student, Herbert George,
Drinking deep from wells of knowledge,
Shall sing of the shape of things to come,
Of animals become men,
And men become predators and prey,
Of ecological invasion
And the rout of civilization,
And fabian dreams of one world at peace;
And my grandson, Aldous
Shall shout out warnings,
Of false Utopias,
Where industry usurps biology,
And men are mass-produced in factories,
Matter-of-factly manufactured,
Designed ever so rationally,
And caste into a world
Where all things are fit to a T!
And dear, dear Charles,
Your name will be an ism to end all schisms,
And some will think it capital to call it social,
And men will fight and die for you!
It shall be a revolution most glorious, Sir Charles,
With protest entry formations
And pure written pride!
No pope!
No king!
No idols!
Not of tribe, cave, marketplace, or theatre!
Their craven images
Smashed to rubble at your feet!

No gods to serve, Charles,
Just You, our Lord Protector,
Seated upon Your Empirical Throne,
With Theory Crowned, and Sceptred Paradigm,
And all shall hail Thee,
And all shall praise Thy Name,
Our own sweet modern Charlemagne!"

Four fearsome horsemen
Come riding down the road
Hooves striking stones, make a dreadful sound

Galapagos! Galapagos! Galapagos!

Mutation, Competition, Selection, and Extinction
Four names, four riders
But one ghastly noise

Galapagos! Galapagos! Galapagos!

Residing in their grim, equatorial habitat
Emerging one by one
From their island citadel

Galapagos! Galapagos! Galapagos!

Their baleful hound leads the hunt
Relentless beagle
Tracks their prey

Galapagos! Galapagos! Galapagos!

/

Knowing no geological barriers
They are masters
Of all they survey

    Galapagos! Galapagos! Galapagos!

Flying fast as the swiftest finch
Harbingers of doom
Like the albatross

    Galapagos! Galapagos! Galapagos!

Scornful as the mockingbird
Born of fire
Like the mighty iguana

    Galapagos! Galapagos! Galapagos!

With all the rage
Of the volcano
Inexorable as the lava flow

    Galapagos! Galapagos! Galapagos!

Clad in impenetrable armor
In their invulnerable
Tortoise shell

Galapagos! Galapagos! Galapagos!

They scour the four corners
Of the earth
They swim the seven seas

Galapagos! Galapagos! Galapagos!

They fly across all time and space
Feel them breathing
Down your neck

Galapagos! Galapagos! Galapagos!
Galapagos! Galapagos!
Galapagos!

overlife or life over
overlife or life over
overlife lives
over and over again
over and over again
over and over again

life over is over
and over is over is over
over and out
over and out

when it's over
it's over
over here
over there
over and over
everywhere

she is over him
he is over her
over and over again
baby!

oh vertical
or horizontal
all over again
until it's over
it's all over
baby!

overlife lives for
ovaries and testes
ovaries and testes
baby!

overlife lives
le vivre est sur la table
reading from the book of overlife
over and over and over again
close the covers
life over
over and out
over and out

survival or sousvival
undergrowth
underlife
undercovers
under and out
going under
going down
down and out
under and over
over and under
double or nothing
going under
going down
drowning in the pool of life
eugene!

overlife lives
over and over and over again
replication
reproduction
reincarnation
recycle
revival
over and over and over again

overlife lives

overlife or life over
overlife or life over

that which survives
survives

and that which does not
does not

and that is all

over and out

I went down to the diner—saw you sittin' there
        down to the diner—saw you sittin' there
turned around for just one minute and

    you disappeared

I went down to the diner—sore 'n' achin',
                        got no prayer
        down to the diner—sore 'n' achin',
                        got no prayer
of ever seein' you again and

    Lord knows my time is near

I went down to the diner—source of food,
                        water, air
        down to the diner—source of food,
                        water, air
don't know what hit the place but

    it's something evil, I do fear

I sat down at your table
but my seat was all wet
spilled a cup of water
and they still ain' mopped it yet
deep fryers are overflowin'
smell of oil fills my head
the staff here ain' good for nothin'
they don' care if we get fed
outside they're gunnin' the engines
of their hot rods an' their bikes
inside they're actin' like sheep
waitin' 'til the butcher strikes
it's the twenty-third solemn day
and it's shadow that they feel
darkness fills the valley
and the past you're knowin' ain' real
so I went down to the diner
to order my last meal

I went down to the diner—saw you sittin' there
        down to the diner—saw you sittin' there
turned away for just one minute and

        you disappeared

Old Farmer Gregor planted his seed
Old Father Gregor followed his creed

crossing hybrids
crossing himself

celebrates their reproduction
celibate in his devotion

records their heredity
recites his Hail Mary

discovers their dominants
prays to his Domini

identifies their recessives
fingers his Rosary

isolates their alleles
praises his Almighty

describes their genetics
confesses to his Jesus Christus

Farmer Gregor will mend all
his socks
in the night
when there's nobody there

Father Gregor has men dole
their wages
to render unto their lords
and their Lord

Singing, *peas porridge hot*
peas porridge cold
peas porridge in the pot
nine days old

He cannot see, hear, smell, taste, or touch them
their genes
his God

But faith and reason will suffice for him
for his principles of peas
for his Prince of Peace

Singing, *some like it hot*
some like it cold
and some like it in the pot
nine days old

she's selective, don't you know?
it's only natural, don't you know?
it's only fitting!

she'll pick and she'll chose
so much to gain, so much to lose
when she plays the mating game

and she'll decide
based on who can best provide
it's only natural!

and whenever she'll consent
to follow the line of descent
from virginity to maternity

she'll come into her own
as she's nesting in her home
as the maiden becomes the mother of eternity!

holy holy matrimony
with this ring
I thee wed!

holy holy mater-moany
with this ring
I thee bed!

sacrament of sex
mixing/matching/recombining
making a production out of reproduction!

choose with wisdom
choose with care
or maybe just whoever's there?

whomever she selects
it's only natural, only fitting
for survival begins and ends with her!

out of the pool, flowing through, swimming
upstream, spawning true, floating down
the birth canal, here comes the offspring!

Great Mother
Mother of us all
Goddess/Empress/Queen

Mother Nature/Mother Nurture
Mother Earth/Mother Ocean
Holy Holy Mother of God

Venus Willendorf
Venus Genetrix
Danu/Nerthus/Frigg

Gaia/Isis/Ninhursag
Durga/Devi/Maya/Mai
Chava/Eve/Lilith/Lucy

Miriam/Mary
The Good Lady Madonna
And Mighty Mighty Mitochondria

Mater
Matrix
Metropolis

Mother City
Mother Land
Mother and Country (and Adam's Apple Pie)

Mother Tongue
Mother Board
(here comes the) Mother Load!

from sacred prostitution
to immaculate conception
she's the source of competition

it's her intelligent design
to make them preen
and make them sweat

it's a matter of selection
gestation and maturation
survival and transformation

she's the Virgin/Mother/Crone
it's only fitting, don't you know?
it's only natural!

Watson, come here, I need you
        I seem to have this crick in my neck
from gazing up at this stairway to heaven
        this spiraling ladder divine

Watson, come here, I want to see you
        for I fear that I may go blind
I have stared into the face of the Godhead
        and unraveled the secret of Life

Watson, come here, it's elementary
        and the base elements' number are few
Adenine, Cytosine, Guanine, and Thymine
        four horsemen come writing on the wall

Watson, come here, it's all quite noble
        it's Adam and Eve joined by a rib
it's Jacob wrestling the angel
        it's self-replicating Diana Parthenos

Watson, come here, I must be frank
        for I no longer know who I am
I've seen these molecular mechanisms mate
        could this be the chemistry of love?

Watson, come here, I need a drink
        make it a double elixir, if you please
I've followed their random recombinant dance
        but I don't know the source of the beat

Watson, come here, please help me
        for now the Bible of Biology's mine
I've decoded that script so very sacred
        and read from the Book of Genetics

Watson, come here, I grow dizzy
        from tracing these curves back and forth
our origins lies back on this corkscrew path
        our destiny lies somewhere up ahead

Deus ex ribo
New clay's breath
A sign?

And so it happened to be
that fate and accident alike
saw us gathering at the station
and huddling close, one and all
waiting for the last train to arrive
anxious to catch the last ride out of town
wanting to make that final getaway
on the Number Ten line
on the train they call
Old Thunder

I saw Watson there
heading for a phone booth
he called his good friend Francis to come down
and together they waited entwined
what a pair!

I saw Father Gregor there
chanting a prayer
that his Lord have mercy on us all

I saw Thomas Henry there
accompanied by Aldous and Henry George
with old Charles seated quite regally
in his wheelchair

I saw Great Mother there
and many lesser mothers too
circulating with compassion and concern

I saw four horsemen ride down and dismount
and wait silently with the crowd
gazing up at the charred coal clouds
and flashes of electric blue
Vulcan-forged
Jovian-hurled
Gaia-piercing
one struck the old family tree
and the ash came crashing through the roof
of the diner
bringing it down
pease porridge poured all over the patrons

I saw Ty ranting on the crystal radio
that he cobbled together on the run:
time to stop monkeying around, he said
when it's over, it's over
over and out
over and out

I saw Judge Scopes come down
from the courthouse
and find his way into the midst of the gathering
he left the jury hung on his gal Lois' humor
declared it a mistrial and error
close-packed
suit-case closed
dismissed and adjourned
it's not my fault, he whispered softly
the Law wasn't written by me

I saw Stephen Jay pointing a finger
at some goo, old, primal, alive
he said,
are you feeling lucky to be punctuated?
is it a period?
an exclamation or interrogative?
or are you looking for an instant comma
a colonoscopy
or just a kissed ellipsis?
it's all equilibrium lost
and equilibrium regained
satiation reigns inhaling
better than in heavy servitude
you know, finding the origin of life
may be the death of me yet

I heard Father Teilhard speak
of God's evolving creation of man
and I heard Doctor Dawkins discuss
man's evolving creation of God
while the monkeys leapt and sang about
the last train to author C. Clarksville
as an orchestra played *Also Sprach*
and Stanley sat in his director's chair
filming these final moments of
a journey through time and space
I'll leave it for the audience to decide, he said
I won't spell out what it all means
I'm just a poor boy from the Bronx
I'm just a simple painter of dreams

I heard Kurt say he wanted a nugget
of a novel idea galloping on
that the simple shall inherit the earth
while complexities vanish
into the tar pits of time

I heard Mother Mary saying
should he shell out some coins
from the purse he carries blithely around?
for I won the bet with a story
of thunder that gave electrical birth
to offspring, a nightmarish breed
I am galvanized by my triumphant tale
of the evil that men do when they defy
Mother Nature's maternal labors

I saw sweet Jane making gorilla talk
saying,
it's good always to recall
how humble in origin we are
the glory of apes in the mystery of ages unfolding
we must love our neighboring species
as ourselves

I saw Rachel spring forth in silence
full grown, born from the strange foam
she was covered in carcinomas
saying,

I am no Cassandra
I've seen it all in my dreams
I've seen the danger
the disappearance
the destruction
catastrophe is coming
can't you tell?
I'll take that last train no matter the destination
whither thou goest I will go too

I heard Sojourner preaching to inquirers
saying,
the truth seems quite clear to me
assuming your personal evolution
has given you eyes that can see
we must all sit down as one species
as we face up to the final Judgment Day

I saw old Karl get on a soapbox
making his marks as he spoke:
I think it's a capital suggestion
to look for transformations
when the means of production
are subject to progressions
as populations are the object
of unnatural oppressions
leading inevitably to revolutions
resulting in mass extinctions

ja, ja, I heard old Sigmund shout back
ja, ja, mein freund, it's true
the ego thinks it's super to keep a lid on the id
we see the return of the repressed
in the dreaming suppressed
advancing from oral to anal
and progressing on to the genital
moving forward by means analytical
consciousness itself can evolve

I saw Ivan feeding meat to his dogs
his voice sounded clear as a bell:
our environment establishes the conditions
through punishments and rewards
we are programmed by natural selections
to be what we eat
to be how we eat
to be where and when as well

I saw Marshall nodding in agreement
saying, *we're sending and extending ourselves*
orbiting in a global embrace
we have become our own mediations
but what is the message of life?
(Neil and Walter echoed the question)
What is the message of life?

I saw Albert sitting at a table
eying a stein of light beer
he said,
no dice, weisenheimer!

all that exists in this universe are relations
it's obvious, just do the math
we are all just energy dynamic
flowing through the unified field
through spacetime together as one

Pablo twirled a mustachio and grinned
Pick a sober man to see movement
Pick a sober man to see change
Pick a sober man to understand
nature is an art form, he said

Salvador dallied a bit, quoting Karl
saying, all that is solid melts away
even time itself is melting down
melting down
melting down
melting down in entropic decay

and I heard good King James shout out
rejoice one and all!
we are witness to translation's transformation
and riders on rapid transition's transmission
revel in the thunders and come circle round
just as all that blooms must one day wither
so new offspring will spawn from every end
swimming upstream to a consciousness risen
here we go loop-de-loo loop-de-lie
just say yes, is that not right sweet Charles?

and I saw everyone turn
and I heard them all quiet down
as old Charles slowly rose to his feet
his frail body swaying unsteady
as he spoke in majestic baritone:

this train has two destinations
two and only two directions
evolution and extinction
evolution and extinction is all
and it is written that there shall be
ten thunders of evolution
ten great leaps forward in history
and it is written that there shall be
ten thunders of extinction
ten events of grim consequence
are they the same ten thunders?
perhaps, perhaps they are
no one knows for certain
no one knows
no one knows

and with that
old Charles sat down

and I was waiting at the station, babe
I was waiting there for you
saying
  Shazam now
  let's transform now
saying it ten times over now:
saying what Thee
safer wrote
  of Sovereignty and Foundation
  of Splendor, Victory, and Beauty
  of Serenity, Kindness, and Understanding
  of Wisdom, and of Will

so we enumerate the emanations
counting down from ten to one
or counting up and onwards without end
will we renew the gestating techcoon golem
to be born anew anointed one?
will we repair the vessels
heal the world tree
heeding the call divine
of sacred space
and time
and love?
will we delight in gems of new awakening
or cry out for a finish again?

and I saw the writing on the wall
it spelled out
    Di
    Nos
    Aur

and I heard a choir singing
    Allelelujah!
as the genee got out of the bottle
and ran off in a fit shouting
    I will fight no more for heaven!
    No ark lies at rainbow's end!

and I asked
    is there nothing to show
    for all this sounding fury?

and I heard the horn blow
and I saw the walls come down
and I listened as someone cried out:

    is there more to it all than survival?
    is there more to it all than mere chance?
    is there more than random recombination?
    is there more than natural adaptation?
    is there meaning to life as we live it?
    is there meaning, and what does it mean?
    our sciences have no answers to give us
    our religions have too many answers to tell

and I saw the train pull into the station
the last train now arrived
and we have to go
we have no choice
it's the last train
and there are no more
and I heard the conductor call out
all aboard
he shouted
all aboard
it's the last call from the station
all aboard the train
he said

and then I saw you there, babe
at the station
you were lost in the crowd
just like me
and you saw me there
from a distance
you saw me there
through the crowd
and we moved
across the gathering
through the crowd
and towards each other
as the conductor called out

all aboard the train now!
all aboard!

and everyone boarded the train
the last train
the very last train
and we tried to reach each other, babe
across the crowd boarding the train
the very last train out of town
we tried to reach each other
as the last train left the station
the last train
out of town

DRAMATIS PERSONAE

THE STORYTELLER, a soul journeyman previously stationed at Terrapin, now owner and proprietor of Rick's Diner

TY, a player

ILSA, a lost love, addressed only as babe

GAIA, a mother and a lover

THE MONKEYS, a rock and roll family group of singers and swingers who find themselves up a tree and out on a limb

THE GRAVE MOTHER, the final score

CHARLES, an English scientist, taxonomist, and theoretician of great renown and revolutionary import

THOMAS HENRY, a British bulldog of sorts and close associate of Charles

HERBERT GEORGE, an English speculative fiction writer and social critic

ALDOUS, a British satirist, novelist, and mystic who ventured through the doors of perception

THE FOUR HORSEMEN, a gaggle of Ecuadorian
gauchos of apocalyptic revelation

EUGENE, an axecutioner

DINER FOLK, a crowd of extras working for scale
and just hanging out

GREGOR, a Silesian scientist and august gardener
known for playing monkish in the middle

THE MOTHERS, an assembly of mistresses of
invention and necessity:

> GREAT MOTHER, an archetypical matriarch,
> forever Jung at heart
>
> MOTHER NATURE, the materfamilias of whom
> it's said that it's not nice to fool her
>
> MOTHER NURTURE, a matron, maternal by
> instinct
>
> MOTHER EARTH, a soiled but fertile hippy type
>
> MOTHER OCEAN, a MILF, wet and wild
>
> MOTHER OF GOD, an immaculate conceiver

VENUS WILLENDORF, a big old mama of
Austrian descent

VENUS GENETRIX, a Roman woman of great
love and beauty, giving birth by Caesarian
section

DANU, a wild Irish mom, source of much singing
and delight

NERTHUS, a German mutter about whom many
mutter in whispered awe and sentimental
schmaltz

FRIGG, a queenly Norse momma, wed unto old
one-eye

ISIS, an Egyptian mummy known for her
brotherly love

NINHURSAG, a Sumerian mountain mama

DURGA, another mountain momma, this one of
Hindu origin

DEVI, the main Hindu mammy

MAYA, a mother of enlightenment, based on a
late night bhoody call

MAI, a Siberian mum obviously less frigid than her reputation would imply

CHAVA, the Hebrew mother of life, married to the red earth

EVE, a mom who knew how to take a ribbing, and raise a little cain

LILITH, a she-devil and lady of the night who got pregnant at an early age

LUCY, a missing link of Australian origin

MIRIAM, a mother of exiles

MARY, a mother in the manger

LADY MADONNA, a mother having trouble making ends meet

MIGHTY MITOCHONDRIA, a maternal microbe

VIRGIN/MOTHER/CRONE, a female trinity, aka, The Supremes

WATSON, an American molecular biologist known for talking on the phone for hours on end whilst playing with the telephone coil

FRANCIS, Watson's partner

JUDGE SCOPES, a jurist of no small prudence (and no relation to John)

THE JURY, twelve hangry men

LOIS, the judge's gal Friday, Saturday, and Sunday, the clerk can't get over her crypt o' night sense of humor

STEPHEN JAY, a popular paleontologist

FATHER TEILHARD, a Jesuit

DOCTOR DAWKINS, an atheist

AUTHOR C. CLARKSVILLE, a geostationary Sri Lankan of far reaching scientific imagination

STANLEY, a filmmaker from New York City

KURT, an American novelist unstuck in time

MARY, an English writer and galvanized mother of a monster

JANE, a British dame, noted follower of the apean way

RACHEL, an American ecologist and environmentalist extraordinaire

SOJOURNER, an American advocate for the human race

KARL, a German economist

SIGMUND, an Austrian therapist

IVAN, a Russian dog whisperer and ringer of chimes

MARSHALL, a Canadian media guru

NEIL, an American teacher, mailman, and follower of Marshall

WALTER, an American Jesuit, past president of the Modern Language Association and former student of Marshall

ALBERT, a Jewish physicist

PABLO, a Spanish artist

SALVADOR, another Spanish artist

KING JAMES, an Irish poet, novelist, and tenfold thunderer

THE GENEE, an escaped prisoner exhibiting bottled up rage and fantasies of wish fulfillment

THE CONDUCTOR, a trained professional with a
  final calling

ABOUT THE AUTHOR

Lance Strate is a native New Yorker, having been born in Manhattan, and moved out to Queens two weeks later, and now working in the Bronx and living in New Jersey, just across the Hudson in SopranoLand. He writes. A lot. Well, not as much as some, but still, quite a bit. His poetry has been published in *Poetica Magazine, KronoScope, Anekaant, ETC, Explorations in Media Ecology, General Semantics Bulletin,* and several anthologies, including *Candy* (which he wrote the introduction for as well), and *The Medium is the Muse: Channeling Marshall McLuhan* (a collection of creative work that he co-edited and also wrote the introduction for). He has written comedy and humor for a zine and local access cable program, lay sermons and prayers, an episode of the nationally syndicated children's animated television program *Adventures of the Galaxy Rangers,* several multimedia presentations, and many blog posts, especially for his own *Blog Time Passing,* and his *BlogVersed* (sadly melted into the air along with the original MySpace social networking site). Lance is perhaps best known for his many essays, well over a hundred of them, that have been published as journal articles and book chapters in edited volumes. And he has a few books of the intellectual sort to his credit, *Echoes and Reflections* is one, *On the Binding Biases of Time* is another, and *Amazing Ourselves to Death* is his most recent. There are some academic anthologies that he has co-edited as well, including *The Legacy of McLuhan,* and he is an editor at NeoPoiesis Press. Lance is a teacher and enjoys his time in the classroom, his formal title being Professor of Communication and Media Studies at Fordham University, and he also teaches in the graduate program in Media and Professional Communication at Fairleigh Dickinson University. He is often identified as a media ecologist, and quite happy to be known as such, having been the founder and first president of the Media Ecology Association. A member of the Board of Trustees of the Institute of General Semantics, and President of Congregation Adas Emuno of Leonia, New Jersey, Lance hopes someday to find the time...

Acknowledgements

I would like to thank my NeoPoiesis colleagues, Dale Winslow, Stephen Roxborough, and Erin Badough, for all of their efforts in making this book possible. Thank you as well to Milo Duffin for his work on the layout, and to Sheffield Abella for the extraordinary cover art.

My gratitude also goes out to Paul Levinson, Si Philbrook, Mickie Harris, Robert Priest, Maria Kontaxis, Lana Deym Campbell, Marty Friedman, Scott Robinson, Mordy Eskononts, Ed Wachtel, and to the many friends, near and far, old and new, online and off, who provided encouragement and inspiration for my (re)turn to poetry. I should also acknowledge the influence of Eric McLuhan in my decision to follow the Joycean ten thunders motif.

I am also grateful to Fordham University, whose motto, Sapientia et Doctrina, which means wisdom and knowledge, speaks to the questions and concerns at the heart of this set of poems, and to Congregation Adas Emuno of Leonia, New Jersey, where the reconciliation of faith and reason through study and spirituality is a never-ending quest.

And many many thanks to my family, my wife Barbara, my son Benjamin, my daughter Sarah, and my mother, Betty Strate.

NeoPoiesis: *a new way of making*

1) in ancient Greece, poiesis referred to the process of making: creation - production - organization - formation - causation

2) a process that can be physical and spiritual, biological and intellectual, artistic and technological, material and teleological, efficient and formal

3) a means of modifying the environment and a method of organizing the self, the making of art and music and poetry, the fashioning of memory and history and philosophy, the construction of perception and expression and reality

4) an independent publisher with a steadfast goal to print and promote outstanding poets, writers and artists that reflect the creative drive and spirit of the new electronic landscape

NeoPoiesisPress.com

www.ingramcontent.com/pod-product-compliance
Lightning Source LLC
LaVergne TN
LVHW091231080426
835509LV00009B/1238